PRAISE FOR

WITHDRAWN

★ "Unique in its coverage of Paralympians, and inspirational on so many levels, this is a great addition for middle school collections."
—*Booklist*, starred review

"Even readers who are not sports enthusiasts will appreciate Long's upbeat account of finding confidence in the water and in life."
—*Kirkus Reviews*

"Her writing style is very engaging, lively, and conversational."
—*School Library Journal*

unsinkable

FROM RUSSIAN ORPHAN TO
PARALYMPIC SWIMMING WORLD CHAMPION

By Jessica Long
With Hannah Long

HOUGHTON MIFFLIN HARCOURT
BOSTON   NEW YORK

For information about permission to reproduce selections from this book, write to trade.permissions@hmhco.com or to Permissions, Houghton Mifflin Harcourt Publishing Company, 3 Park Avenue, 19th Floor, New York, New York 10016.

hmhbooks.com

The text was set in Neutraface 2 Text.

The Library of Congress has cataloged the hardcover edition as follows:
Names: Long, Jessica Tatiana, author. | Long, Hannah, author.
Title: Unsinkable: from Russian orphan to paralympic swimming world champion / by Jessica Long, with Hannah Long.
Description: Boston, Massachusetts : Houghton Mifflin Harcourt, [2018] | Includes bibliographical references and index.
Identifiers: LCCN 2018000945 (print) | LCCN 2017041724 (ebook)
Subjects: LCSH: Long, Jessica Tatiana,—Juvenile literature. | Swimmers—United States—Biography—Juvenile literature. | Athletes with disabilities—United States—Biography—Juvenile literature.
Classification: LCC GV838.L65 (print) | LCC GV838.L65 A3 2018 (ebook) | DDC 797.2/1092 [B] —dc23
LC record available at https://lccn.loc.gov/2018000945

ISBN: 978-1-328-70725-3 hardcover
ISBN: 978-0-358-23837-9 paperback

Manufactured in China
SCP 10 9 8 7 6 5 4 3 2 1
4500791215

For my hero: my dad, Steve Long.
you were the first person who said
I should have a book one day.
Thanks for always, always believing in me.

contents

introduction

LIFE-CHANGING MOMENTS. Many people can point to a time when they had one of these moments . . . or maybe two or three. They're faced with an event that shifts their whole world and makes them look at things differently. I can't say for sure how many of these most people have in a lifetime, but my life has definitely been filled with them. As a double amputee who was born in Siberia, was adopted by an American family, and spent more than a decade as a competitive swimmer, I can point to any number of moments that have altered the course of my life. Some of those moments have been obvious ones, broadcasted to the world by media outlets. Some were small, quiet ones that I struggled through. But all had an impact on my life, shaping who I am today. When I thought about writing a book about my story, it made sense to talk about all of them. I hope that in sharing my journey, I can show that we don't have to let our circumstances define us. I certainly could never have planned—or even imagined—the way in which my life has unfolded so far, but I wouldn't change my unique experiences. We never know which moments are the ones that will lead to a new opportunity or will touch someone else's life.

So here they are, my life-changing moments . . .

THE MOMENT I WON MY FIRST GOLD

did not come here to be second. The water blocks out every sound, and I feel my heartbeat pulsing with each stroke of my arms. I glance over again to see the feet of my competitor, which means I'm still behind her. *I did not come here to be second!* This is my last thought before throwing every ounce of energy into flying toward the other end of the pool, slicing through the water, and reaching for the wall at the same moment she does. I turn to the scoreboard to see who won, but I can't fully make out the names through my fogged-up goggles. I briefly process that my competitor doesn't look very celebratory, and then I see it. Next to the number 1, "Jessica Long" is listed at the top. I hesitantly throw my arm in the air and smile as cameras go off. I can't believe it. That's me. I'm gasping for air, gripping the wall to keep myself above the surface because I'm too exhausted to tread water, but that's MY NAME on the board!

I am Jessica Long, and that was the moment I won my first gold medal in the hundred-meter freestyle at the Paralympic Games in Athens, Greece.

I've never been good at listening to people. They always seem to tell me what I can't do, which I see as merely an opinion until I've tried it to my full capacity. I want to hear what I *can* do. I remember sitting in the hotel room at the Paralympic Trials, my dad preparing me for the possibility of my not making the team. He was laying out some facts about how young I was, and how new I was to the world of competitive swimming, telling me there was plenty of time to train for the next round of games. I was twelve years old, and I looked him dead in the eye and said,

Listening to my national anthem play on the podium at the Athens Games.
Nothing can fully describe this moment.

"I'm going to make the team. I know I am." Sure enough, they called my name, making me the youngest athlete on the U.S. Paralympic team in any sport.

When I was growing up, even if my parents were giving me a rule for my own benefit and protection, I immediately wanted to go against it. I'm sure it was frustrating for them, but that's the way I needed to live my life—to face everything I was up against. That's the determination that got me to Athens.

FAVORITE QUOTES:
"NO ONE IS YOU, AND THAT IS YOUR POWER."
"BE SO GOOD THEY CAN'T IGNORE YOU."

Everything surrounding my time in Athens excited me. Rolling into the Olympic Village with the rest of the U.S. swim team, I was amazed by what I saw. I became best friends with three of the girls living in my building. Kelly, Casey, Elizabeth, and I dubbed ourselves the Four Mousekateers, and I was known as the housekeeper of the group because I was constantly tidying our suite. I was in awe of everything all the older swimmers did. I watched the seventeen-year-olds put on makeup, thinking they were the absolute coolest. I didn't have any makeup, as I wasn't allowed to wear it yet, so I may have used one of their eyeliners when they weren't around . . .

I loved the freedom I had on that trip. Since I was homeschooled and constantly with my family, it was as if I were having my first college experience. I grew up a bit in those three weeks, finding my independence, having the time of my life, feeling like a little adult. And on top of that, I was there to swim!

Waking up in the village on the day of my first race, I was a bundle of nerves. All I could manage to eat for breakfast was a banana. I boarded the bus to head over to the pool, did my pre-race warm-up, got on my tiny racing suit, and waited. Waiting was the worst part. As a twelve-year-old, I just wanted to race. Finally it was my turn. I walked to the call room, showed them my credentials, and proceeded to line up. Suddenly the nerves were gone. I was ready. My first race in competition was the hundred-meter freestyle preliminaries, for which several heats would race and the fastest eight swimmers would advance to the finals later that night. When I touched the wall in the prelims and the coach told me my time, I knew that put me first in the world. I didn't get too excited, because I knew that the seasoned athletes hold back in order to qualify in the prelims and then up their game for the finals. I was seeded first for that evening, so I was lined up to swim in the fourth lane (the fastest swimmers are in lanes four and five—the center lanes). With my strong finish in the preliminaries, my coach and my family thought I might be able

Sitting in the stands with my dad after winning my first Paralympic gold medal.

to win the bronze medal, but I had this crazy desire to win gold. The gun went off, I dove in, and 1:08.86 minutes later, I won my first gold medal in the Paralympics!

Lining up for the medal ceremony, I didn't fully grasp the significance of what was happening. It was finally settling into my mind that I had won. My USA gear was too big for my frame, and I had thrown my wet hair into a haphazard ponytail. I wasn't wearing makeup or thinking about the photographs; I was busy taking in the moment. We walked out to the podium, and I thought *Don't trip* as I walked forward to receive the gold medal. I threw my hand up in a fist and smiled. As our national anthem started to play and the flags were raised, I took a second to remind myself which hand was my right one, pulled the wreath from my hair, and placed it over my heart. I honestly didn't even know the entire national anthem, but I mouthed pieces of it and grinned through the rest, completely amazed by the moment. My place on that podium was proof to me that I could do anything I put my mind to. I had said I would be up there, and there I was, my national anthem playing and my face up on the screen. I could hear Team USA close by in the stands, and I was so proud to be representing my country and my fellow athletes.

This was the moment when I knew there was absolutely nothing stopping me from being the best. Swimming was a wonderful outlet for channeling all my emotions. The pool was my home, I knew that, but this was different. Here I was, the youngest Paralympian on the U.S. team, and I just received a gold medal. I still didn't fully comprehend the impact of what I had just done, but I knew that I liked it, and I wanted to repeat it. I went on to win two more gold medals in Athens. I was overjoyed! I loved swimming. I loved competing. And as it turned out, I loved winning.

In swimming, classifications are divided into three groups: S1 through S10 competitors are those with physical impairment. An S1 will have the most severe impairment and an S10 a lesser impairment. Athletes are judged on their muscle strength, joint range of motion, limb length, and movement coordination. S11 through S13 swimmers are those with visual impairment. S14 is for athletes with learning difficulties. Depending on their disability and how it fluctuates (e.g., some paralysis and injuries can heal, while other conditions are degenerative), some competitors have to be continuously reclassified. I compete as an S8 in freestyle, backstroke, and butterfly, and as an SB7 in breaststroke (the B literally just stands for breaststroke). Swimmers in this classification are described as having "full use of their arms and trunk with some leg function; swimmers with coordination problems mainly in the lower limbs; both legs amputated just above or just below the knee; single above elbow amputation." I am a below-the-knee, bilateral amputee. I will forever remain an S8, without reclassification, as obviously my legs can't grow back.

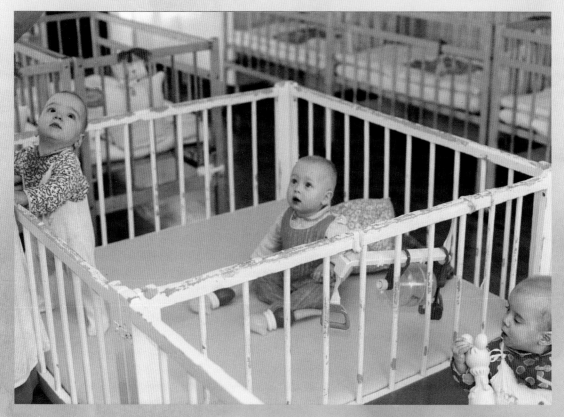

My home for the first thirteen months of my life.

2

THE MOMENT I BECAME
A LONG

Secondary infertility. That's what the doctors said it was called. My parents, with two healthy children, were told they could never biologically have more. They walked out of that office and immediately looked to adoption, something they had discussed already, to add to their family. They started taking classes offered by Associated Catholic Charities, where they learned all about adoption and what the possibilities were, and they were connected with helpful agencies and social workers. My soon-to-be mom heard about a little girl in Russia who had problems with her legs and was up for adoption. My parents say they didn't set out specifically to adopt children with special needs, but they hadn't ruled it out, either. They knew that a lot of overseas orphans had physical disabilities, and they had checked to make sure their health insurance covered any surgeries, hospital visits, and so on that might be necessary. They were prepared to open their home and help however they could. So, following this lead, they got in touch with a group of people who had helped some families adopt children from Russia and were putting together another group to adopt from the same orphanage. My parents learned more about this little girl with malformed legs and were shown their first picture.

My mom says she knew right away that this was the child God wanted them to adopt. My parents always wanted a total of four children, including the two they already had, so they decided to adopt a second child from the same orphanage. In December 1992, Steve and Beth Long made plans to adopt a little boy,

Dennis Alekseevich Tumashoff, along with the little girl, Tatiana Olegovna Kirillova.

They began the journey with paperwork and background checks, collecting letters of reference, and answering questions about how they grew up and what future plans they had for their family. Multiple visits to their home were required, too. These home studies are an in-depth examination of the house and surroundings in which an adoptee would grow up. In order to raise funds, the Longs sold a number of items, including the twelve-passenger van they had used for a daycare center they formerly operated. They requested more information on their Russian children in an attempt to prepare for what surgeries would be needed, but they were provided with no medical history. The only information my future parents had was a picture of me and my legs, along with the knowledge that Dennis had a cleft lip and palate. Desperate for more information about us, they even took the picture of me to a specialist at Johns Hopkins Hospital to see if he could tell them anything more, but nothing could be determined without x-rays and a medical history. Incredibly,

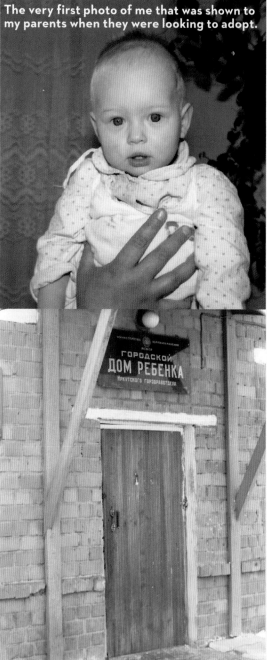

The very first photo of me that was shown to my parents when they were looking to adopt.

The door to the orphanage Josh and I were in. The building was decrepit, and the windows and doors let in a draft.

it took less than three months from the moment they decided to adopt us to the moment my dad boarded the plane for Russia. Because they already had two kids, my mom stayed home in Baltimore to care for them. My dad would take the long trip solo, during two weeks away from his job, to bring us to our new home.

Steve Long's first trip outside the United States took him halfway around the world to meet the newest members of his family. He flew out of Dulles International Airport with a group of other parents who were adopting, and after a layover in Shannon, Ireland, they landed in Moscow. From there, he flew to Irkutsk, where the orphanage was located. I can't imagine what he must have been feeling, walking into that orphanage, knowing his daughter was inside, seeing me amid all the other children, locking eyes with me—his little girl—for the first time. He. Chose. Me!

It took me the longest time to understand this, though my parents told me about it frequently. Some parents are introduced to their new child on a sonogram screen and then meet her in a hospital room after nine months of careful preparation. But my remarkable parents were introduced to their new child through a photograph, and, moved by her story, they agreed to meet her for the first time in a foreign country, surrounded by strangers who did not speak their language. Still, I was *their* child, loved wholly and beyond reason. I get it now. He was there for me. Yeah, he was there for my brother*, too... but right now we are talking about my story, okay?

Josh and me.

My dad tells some of the best stories about the return trip from Russia with the two newest additions of his family in tow. Little did he know, a blizzard dubbed the "storm of the century" was blowing in and would cause our plane to land in Canada, where we would be stranded overnight. Suddenly, taking care of a three-year-old and a thirteen-month-old in a different country seemed daunting. Between my brother puking on the plane, me

Once in the U.S., I met the requirements for citizenship and nothing else technically had to be done. But my parents decided to go through the formal process and get me an official Certificate of Citizenship.

continuously rolling over the pillow fortress my dad had built and falling off the hotel bed, and running out of diapers . . . we definitely had some great bonding time. To me, that trip symbolizes the craziness these two little Russian orphans continuously brought to our parents' lives, but I'm told we were worth it.

My family never treated me differently because I was adopted. My new older sister was ecstatic to have another girl around (before she realized I would grow up to steal her things), and my brother was always my protector (he's a police officer now). My name was changed from Tatiana Olegovna Kirillova to Jessica

Stranded in Canada for the night.

Tatiana Long, and my parents' perfect family of six was complete . . . or so they thought. My mom miraculously got pregnant again three years later . . . and then again two years after that, giving me two little sisters and a total of five siblings.

When Dennis Alekseevich Tumashoff was adopted, my parents changed his name to Joshua Dennis Long. We were not biologically related; we just happened to be in the same orphanage. Though Josh is two years older than I am, everyone at home thought we were twins at first. He was malnourished and had spent many months in a Russian hospital, suffering with dysentery, so his tiny body was as small as my thirteen-month-old frame. Shortly after his adoption, his cleft lip and palate were repaired. Over the years, he has gone through a series of surgeries, including extensive reconstruction of his jaw. Unlike me, he has never had an interest in searching for information about his birth parents.

Holding my new little sister, Hannah.

Two Russians in the woods, a year after our adoption.

Taking a quick nap on my mom while on family vacation, about one month after being adopted.

All smiles with my two oldest siblings, Amanda and Steven.

3

THE MOMENT I LEARNED
TO WALK WITH PROSTHESES

Just a few months after we got back from Russia, the hospital visits started. I was born with fibular hemimelia, a birth defect in which all or part of the fibular bone is missing. I didn't have ankles, heels, or most of the bones in my lower legs. One in forty thousand babies are born with this defect every year. The cause is unclear. The defect usually occurs in only one leg—the right fibula more often than the left—but both of mine were compromised. It looked like my bones didn't continue to grow beyond a few inches below my knee, though I did have a small foot, with three toes on each leg. After consulting several specialists, my parents were advised that the best choice for someone with my severity of fibular hemimelia was amputation, just below the knee. This would allow me to be fitted with prosthetics and eventually learn to walk.

My mom says that the night before my surgery was really hard for her. My family loved every part of me, including my little half-formed feet that were going to be amputated, but they knew it was necessary. My mom cried. She and my dad prayed that I wouldn't experience much pain, that the doctors would be precise and alert, and that my eighteen-month-old self wouldn't feel a loss because of no longer having my feet. The following morning, we drove to Saint Agnes Hospital, where Dr. Robert Bright would perform the surgery. My mom was fighting tears, so my dad held me a lot of the time while we waited.

My grandparents were struggling with emotions too, but I'm told I was happy until the nurses came to take me for the surgery. By then I was starting to get

My baby doll with missing feet just like me.

hungry and fussy, but my mom wasn't allowed to go in with me. Still, my parents made sure to send my little doll with me. They had cut off her feet and bandaged her legs so she would look just like me afterward.

When I woke up in the recovery room, the doll was lying by my side. I could see red poles coming out of the casts wrapped around my legs. They were my first pair of prosthetics, my pole legs. Within twenty-four hours of waking from my amputation, I stood up on that first pair of legs, balancing there in the middle of the children's playroom in the hospital. My parents had made an appointment with a physical therapist, but I was walking around on my prosthetic legs so soon that they canceled it.

Even at such a young age, I knew I could do what everyone else was doing. That determination, along with a fiercely competitive spirit, made everything a race between my siblings and me. Oh, you think you're going to finish your ice cream before me? Guess again. Walking through the door? I will push you out of the way to get inside first. Don't even get me started on board games. If I wasn't good at the game, I didn't want to play it. I was

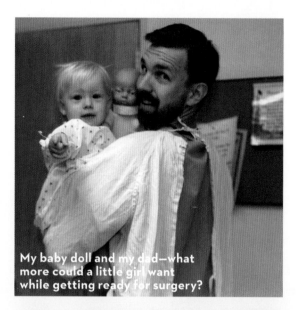

My baby doll and my dad—what more could a little girl want while getting ready for surgery?

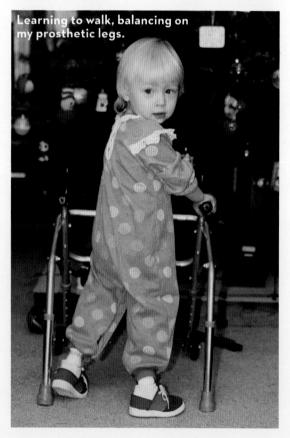

Learning to walk, balancing on my prosthetic legs.

determined to dominate at everything I did.

Climbing on top of the refrigerator was a favorite pastime of mine. I would scramble from the countertops to the fridge and hide behind the cleaning products. I was unbeatable at hide-and-seek. My siblings quickly caught on to my strategy, but it was years before my mom found out that I used to hide up there. It was a daily goal of mine to see how much I could sneak past my mom and how much I could get away with. I'm not sure how she homeschooled six vastly different children while still maintaining a semblance of sanity, but my mom is incredibly kindhearted and strong, and she always encouraged me to try new things and be the best I could be.

I made the daily choice to not let anything hold me back, especially my legs. Now, even when I am too tired or too sore to put on my prosthetics, I still make that choice. I choose to rely on my competitive nature and determination to be as tough as I was after that first surgery. I refuse to let that little girl down by giving in.

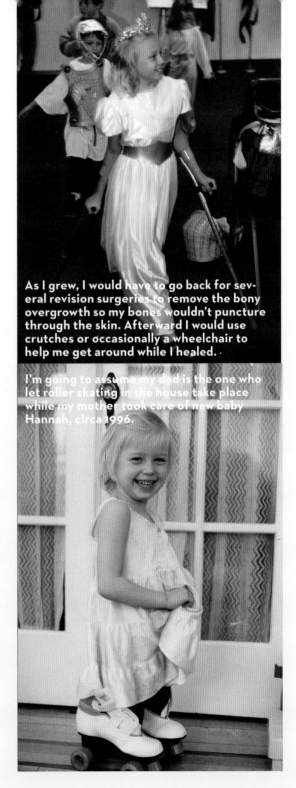

As I grew, I would have to go back for several revision surgeries to remove the bony overgrowth so my bones wouldn't puncture through the skin. Afterward I would use crutches or occasionally a wheelchair to help me get around while I healed.

I'm going to assume my dad is the one who let roller skating in the house take place while my mother took care of new baby Hannah, circa 1996.

Poolside kisses with Momma Long.

4

THE MOMENT I DISCOVERED WATER

More than anything, I love being surrounded by water. Fully immersed in that relentless, translucent, beautiful element, I feel at home. I'm alive there. It gives me a sense of freedom—the freedom of not feeling disabled or limited. I used to say that swimming was my escape, but that's not accurate. Swimming forced me to deal with the things I wanted to escape. It helped me work through a lot of feelings and frustrations, because I had hours under water just to swim laps and think. I had the freedom to be alone with myself, completely unlimited by my circumstances or my body while doing what I loved. I think that's why I took to swimming with such ease. All my life I have had to fight to catch up with people. But not in the water. That's the one place where everyone else is trying to keep up with me!

I've always been an observer. I watch people interact with one another and see how they move through life. When I was younger, I would observe the differences between them and me. Sometimes, when I saw how people had things easier than I did, I envied them. It's hard to describe, but when I look back now, I can see how some people in my situation might have given up. It's easy to get carried away by negative thoughts—that comparison game. But when I found swimming, it was *This is what I've been waiting for.* All those times in recovery from infections or surgeries, wondering why this was my life. I had so many things built up inside of me that I wasn't sure what to do with, and swimming was the key. I found the thing I was made for, and it was a relief.

I wore tights in the gym to help protect my knees from bacteria. My legs can easily become infected if I get a cut.

Working on my balance beam skills as an eight-year-old.

When my prosthetic legs are off, I do everything on my knees. I walk, run, jump, bounce, and play. My parents got me involved in gymnastics when I was four years old as a way to channel my energy into movement. I loved the uneven bars, the trampoline, and flying into the foam pit. I thought doing cartwheels and flips was the coolest.

Unfortunately, my parents worried about the constant pressure on my knees each time I landed. They were afraid I was putting too much pressure on my joints. I still remember the day they sat me down and issued an ultimatum. They told me I could continue with gymnastics if I would try it while wearing my prosthetics, or I could find a new sport that would be gentler to my knees. At the time, my legs were not as advanced as they are now and I relied on a suction system to hold each prosthesis in place. If someone stepped on my foot, I would pop right out of my leg. Imagine trying to do gymnastics while balancing on stilts—constantly afraid that someone will step on your foot and you'll end up on the floor, or worried that a leg might shoot across the room into someone's face while you are doing a flip. I didn't really have much of a choice. I had done gymnastics for six years, and it was hard to say goodbye, but I refused to wear my legs in the gym. So off to the next sport! I tried basketball, cheerleading, ice-skating, skiing, running, and rock climbing. But the thing that stuck was swimming.

I had always loved being in a pool. My family had lunch at my grandparents' house every Sunday after church, and as soon as the weather was warm enough, they opened their pool. I love my grandparents, and visits to their house were always the best. They had cable TV and provided an endless supply of Popsicles and watermelon.

I did gymnastics for six years before making the switch to swimming.

FAVORITE TV SHOWS: *GOSSIP GIRL* AND *GILMORE GIRLS.*

But the best part was my grandparents' peanut-shaped pool. Rain or shine, I was always in that pool. It's where my love for swimming started. For hours upon hours I played mermaid. Alone or with my sisters, I would tie my little legs together and pretend I was lost at sea and had to befriend the dolphins to help me get back home. Or I would throw my necklace into the water and then dive around the pool until I found it. Since mermaids can see underwater, I rarely bothered with goggles. I would stay in the pool until my eyes were bloodshot and my fingers wrinkled. I was always the first one in and the last one out of the water.

When my grandmother read about a local swim team in the newspaper and mentioned it to me, I figured, *Why not?* It was a sport I could do without my prosthetics, and I already knew I loved the water. I joined Dundalk-Eastfield Swim Club (DESC) when I was ten, knowing only two of the four strokes—freestyle and backstroke. On the day of my first practice I was very nervous. I was the only girl without legs, but that wasn't new to me. I jumped into the cold water and did the best I could. The butterfly stroke was explained to me on my first day of practice, but it took me a few days to learn how to pull my body up out of the water without getting a mouthful of chlorine. The first time I did a full lap of butterfly all the way across the pool, I thought I would drown. Thankfully, I'm a fast learner and I pay attention to details, so I picked it up quickly and continued to get stronger and faster. I couldn't help but fall in love with the sport. During practice I felt as if I were on autopilot, as if my mind were a thousand miles away, but my arms kept moving, stroke after stroke. I kept

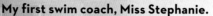

Getting some new bling at the USA Swimming Disability Championships in 2003.

My first swim coach, Miss Stephanie.

Looking to the scoreboard after my swim at the 2004 Paralympic Trials.

going back to swim practice because I loved the feeling of racing, continuously trying to beat my previous time. I enjoyed swimming against the girls with legs, and I thought it was pretty awesome when I could beat them. I technically had a disadvantage with my legs, but I had strong arms, and I was fast.

I thrived on the competition and on being surrounded by other swimmers who encouraged me. I also fell in love with the team and admired how the girls treated me as an equal competitor. They didn't seem to notice that I was missing my legs. In fact, most people didn't realize they were missing until I got out of the pool.

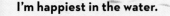
I'm happiest in the water.

5

THE MOMENT I WAS SURROUNDED BY PEOPLE LIKE ME

A little over a year after I started swimming, Linda Sue Lottes, the adaptive swim chairperson for Maryland Swimming, approached my dad and said that I might be fast enough for the Paralympics. At that time, we had never heard of the Paralympics, only the Olympics and Special Olympics. After doing research, we found that the Paralympic Games is the second-largest multi-sporting event in the world—a major international competition for athletes who have a range of physical disabilities. There are twenty-two Summer Paralympic sports, ranging from sitting volleyball to judo to wheelchair basketball . . . to swimming.

The first Paralympic Games was held in Rome in 1960. It was called the Paralympics because it is parallel to the Olympic Games. Paralympians compete two weeks after the Olympics and use all the same venues. Gold, silver, and bronze medals are awarded for first, second, and third place in each event.

Once I learned about the Paralympic Games, I became obsessed with the idea of racing others who were like me. I started training harder than ever in practice. Even at eleven years old, a year out from the 2004 Paralympic Games in Athens, Greece, I set a goal to make that Paralympic Team. When I was eight, after an afternoon of playing mermaid in my grandparents' pool, I took a break and found the rest of my family gathered around the TV. I was curious to know what everyone was watching,

Haven Shepherd is a bilateral amputee like me.
I love being her mentor.

The Long sisters (Amanda, me, Hannah, and Grace) in Athens, Greece. I'm not sure what I would do without my crazy sisters and their constant support.

so I asked. They told me it was the Olympics, where "the best athletes in the world come together and compete for a gold medal." I knew right then and there that I wanted to become an Olympian. Now I knew I could live that dream through the Paralympic Games, and there was nothing I wanted more.

Qualifying for Athens and winning three gold medals in 2004 fulfilled that dream, but there was something about the experience that had even more of an impact on me. As a little girl, I had never seen another double amputee my age. Imagine what that was like for me—never seeing another young girl

Coming up for a breath in my favorite swim stroke, butterfly.

who was missing her legs. Suddenly I was thrust into a world of passionate, inspirational athletes with disabilities. There is nothing quite like being on a pool deck surrounded by other amputees. I didn't have to worry about acceptance or feeling different. It's an exclusive club—you have to be missing an arm or leg to be part of it.

Once I entered the Paralympic world, I was constantly meeting people with paralysis, dwarfism, cerebral palsy, and multiple sclerosis. I met blind athletes, paraplegics, and military vets who had lost limbs overseas. At a Paralympic swim meet you'll find

With my swim coach, Andrew Barranco, who has coached me on and off for my entire career.

Tiny but determined . . . to earn a place on the U.S. Paralympic Swim Team.

wheelchairs and prosthetic arms and legs all around the pool deck. It looks like a war zone. Some prosthetics have fake skin and are painted to look real (I always liked mine to look real), and others are just exposed poles and mechanical parts. It's hard to put into words how incredible it felt to discover that I wasn't alone. It all just felt right.

One of my early idols was Erin "Po" Popovich. She was a competitive swimmer in the S7 classification and the nicest girl I had ever met. She had confidence that was contagious. She was constantly smiling in and out of the pool and was a friend to everyone. I had the opportunity to race her in the SB7 hundred-meter breaststroke. I drop down a class for breaststroke (I'm an S8 in every other stroke), as that one relies more on leg power. Throughout the years we constantly fought each other for the fastest time, always touching the wall in first and second place. I never minded losing to her, though of course I swam my hardest to win. She retired in 2010 after the World Championships.

Every little girl needs a hero, and that's what Erin was for me. In 2012, during the Paralympic Games in London, after she had retired, I won gold in the hundred-meter breaststroke, the event she had won four years earlier in the Beijing Games. We received flowers on the podium, and I knew right away who I wanted to give my flowers to. Po was working as a classifier at the meet, so I left the bouquet and a note on her bed. If she couldn't be on that podium with me, I was determined to share part of it with her.

The Paralympics gave me newfound confidence in my prosthetics when I went back home. I started wearing shorts and showing my knees, no longer caring if everyone knew I didn't have legs. I still found myself getting annoyed when people would stare, but I was more willing to answer kids' questions and explain that I was born this way and it wasn't a big deal. If I'd had legs, I wouldn't be in the Paralympics and wouldn't have met the amazing athletes and made the friends that I had. I felt as if my life had meaning; my "disability" had meaning. I still had hard days, where I was angry and in pain, and I just wanted things to be easier, but now I had people I could call, people who would listen to me vent, who were dealing with the same thing. I had found a second family—a family of intense, beautiful, determined daily warriors . . . just like me.

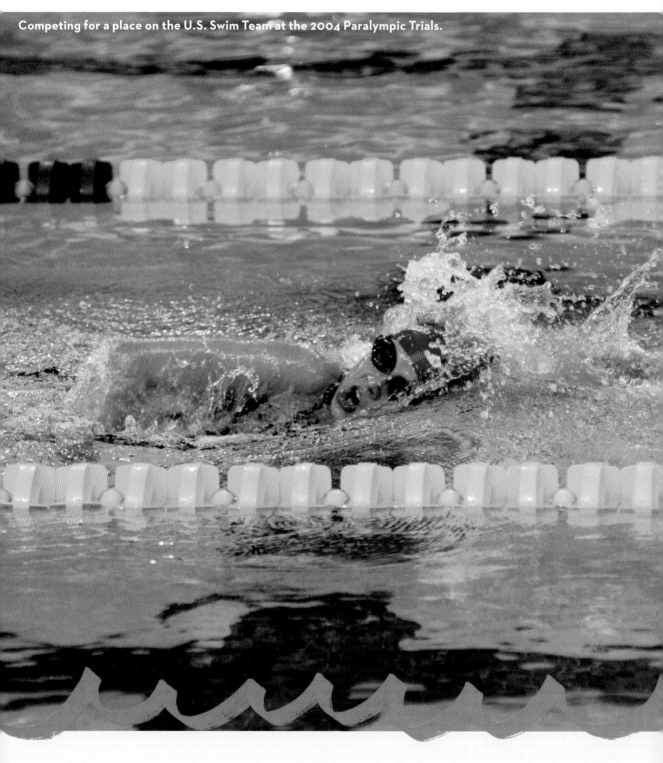

Competing for a place on the U.S. Swim Team at the 2004 Paralympic Trials.

Freestyle event in the 2016 Paralympic Games at the Olympic Aquatics Stadium in Rio De Janeiro, Brazil. Swimming my way to gold in my favorite Arena cap and goggles.

6

THE MOMENT I BECAME A
PROFESSIONAL ATHLETE

It's April 2007, and I'm dressed in a beautiful bright red dress and seated in a fancy auditorium. Suddenly I look around and realize that everyone is looking at me. It takes a second for my brain to process what was just announced. *Oh my gosh, they called my name!* My hands had already lifted to start clapping for the winner, so instead I put them back down awkwardly and pushed myself up out of my seat. I walked to the podium to receive the award I had just won over Michael Phelps, Sasha Cohen, Apolo Ohno, and a bunch of other amazing athletes who had been nominated. The James E. Sullivan Award is presented by the Amateur Athletic Union and is awarded annually to "the most outstanding amateur athlete in the United States." I really went to the dinner in New York City only to meet some of these athletes I so much admired. My dad and sister were my dates for the evening.

WHOM I LOOK UP TO:
STEVE LONG, A.K.A. MY DAD. I
ADMIRE HIM FOR HIS LOVE FOR
OUR FAMILY AND EVERYTHING
HE HAS DONE FOR ME.

Being honored as the recipient of the seventy-seventh Amateur Athletic Union Sullivan Award, presented to the USA's top amateur athlete. I was the first Paralympic athlete to win the award.

I had my dad and sister Hannah there to experience the event and meet the other athletes with me. You can kind of see my smudged makeup from crying after I won.

I remember my dad trying to prep me in case I won, wanting me to be prepared with something to say. I brushed him off as most sassy fifteen-year-olds do, assuming I knew how things would play out.

I wasn't going to win this one. But there I was, walking toward the podium with tears in my eyes (and wishing I had a speech prepared!). I thanked them for honoring me as the first Paralympian to ever win the Sullivan Award, and I stumbled through something about how I just loved to swim. I was so proud to be recognized for my hard work and dedication to the sport.

I was only two years into this Paralympic world, but I was already being recognized because I had just swept the World Championships, winning all nine of my events (seven individual swims and two relays). Being able to participate in parades made me feel important. It was an honor to be interviewed and congratulated after Athens, but this kind of attention was completely different. Nine gold medals were bound to draw some attention, and they most certainly did. Shortly after winning the Sullivan Award, I was approached by Nike. I couldn't believe it. Nike wanted me? I have high expectations for myself, but I never thought

Nike was going to call and say they wanted me to represent them. I had "gone pro" the previous year, when I signed a contract with a management company. Once an amateur athlete signs with a sponsor, she officially becomes a professional athlete and is ineligible for college scholarships related to her sport. My parents and I had discussed it and decided it was worth it. Swimming was my world, and I wanted to see where that could take me. When Nike expressed an interest in me, I knew I had made the right decision. The contracts were signed, and at age fifteen I became a true professional athlete.

One of the best parts was receiving a private account and being able to order all sorts of Nike clothes. My favorite item was a pair of green-and-pink sneakers with zebra stripes on the side. I wore them everywhere. I loved feeling so influential that Nike wanted me to wear its clothes. I loved being linked to a brand and being able to call myself a professional athlete. Since Nike, I have collaborated with several other corporations, including Nutrilite, a vitamin company, as well as Arena swimwear, Liberty Mutual, Oakley, and Airweave. Visa even put my face on a credit card!

Posing next to my picture in a giant Visa ad.

I was selected to work with Coca-Cola as one of eight athletes they chose to represent them for the 2012 Games. I had my very own Coke commercial, which was a blast to shoot. They had to teach me how to drink out of the soda bottle—who knew there was a right way and a wrong way to do it for the camera?

I remember going to a movie theater, shocked to see my face on the screen before the previews began. I modeled for Ralph Lauren, and my picture was on posters all over Macy's and in *Elle* and *Vogue* magazines. My grandmother actually convinced a mall employee to give her one of the displays when they were taking it down. We had a Ralph Lauren display with my face on it gracing our living room for much too long after that.

I can't believe all the companies I've had the privilege to work with and who've helped share my story. I've seen more sponsorship opportunities open up to Paralympians through the years, and it has been an honor helping to spread awareness of the Paralympic movement and to see how it has steadily gained more attention and coverage in the United States. I love that I've been part of it.

Celebrating silver on the podium at the medal ceremony in Rio.

At the Nike suite in Houston, Texas, for team processing, one week before leaving for Rio.

7

THE MOMENT I WON AN ESPY

The ESPY Awards are like the Oscars for sports. In 2007, I received a phone call from my agent, who told me that I was nominated for Best Female Athlete with a Disability! I should mention that these votes are cast by the general public, so my family had sent out lots of emails and posts on social media to vote, vote, vote. Still, it was a big honor to even be nominated. I decided to take my big sister Amanda with me as my date. She is someone I always looked up to, and I knew we'd have a great time together. My mom took us shopping at Nordstrom for gowns. Amanda and I would be walking the red carpet with other athletes and celebrities, so I wanted it to be perfect. I settled for a bright blue silk dress with an open back. I fell in love with it immediately, especially because it showed my strong swimmer's back. The ESPYs are held in Los Angeles, so they flew my sister and me first class, and I felt like a true celebrity. When we got to our hotel room, we found out about the ESPY gift suites. My sister and I went to the third floor, where all kinds of brands had stations set up featuring their clothes and accessories. We walked from room to room, adding gifts to our bag. I remember thinking, *This is all for simply being nominated for an award*? My favorite gifts were a custom pair of True Religion jeans and a pair of Fendi sunglasses, both of which I still own.

After "shopping" the gift suites, we went to the pre-party. This was when I really felt as if I had made it bigtime. There are pre-parties, after-parties, and even an after-after-party at the ESPYs. I knew my chances of meeting celebrities were

We saw Michael Phelps at the 2007 ESPYs and I had to get a picture.

Leaving the ESPYs after-after-party in Los Angeles, California, with my sister Amanda.

really good, but I didn't expect to see one of my favorites. Amanda and I were at the pre-party, laughing and having a great time admiring everyone's clothing and dancing with each other, when my sister made a comment about how funny it would be if we saw Hilary Duff. I kid you not, no more than thirty seconds later I turned around and saw Hilary Duff. I didn't work up the nerve to run over and say hi, but just being in the same room with her meant the world to me. *The Lizzie McGuire Movie* is one of my all-time favorites.

FAVORITE MOVIES: *A LOT LIKE LOVE, TITANIC, TOY STORY, A WALK TO REMEMBER.*

Everything at the ESPYs is designed to make you feel special. The following day, Amanda and I got our hair and makeup done, put on our new attire in our hotel room, and set off to walk the red carpet. When our car arrived at the event, there was a sign directing the attendees and nominees. I was in awe of the whole experience. Amanda knew more of the celebrities than I did, pointing them out to me as we walked. There were so many cameras, and I loved pausing to pose for each one. We took our time on the red carpet, soaking up every minute of it.

I ended up winning that year. Since Best Female Athlete with a Disability is not a televised category, my award wasn't presented live. My name flashed on the screen as the ceremony was on commercial break, but I didn't care. I won! I left the theater to go to the bathroom to call my family and share the good news. The ESPY was later sent to our house, and it had my name engraved on the front of the little plaque. We discovered that the statue is a lot heavier than it looks. That award is something I'm really proud of. A lot of athletes dream of being invited to the ESPYs, and I've had the privilege four times. I won in 2007, 2012, and 2013. I was nominated in 2009, but Erin Popovich won that year. If there's anyone who's allowed to beat me, it's Po. I was so happy for her. I am truly grateful simply to have been at these events with all these incredible athletes.

Running into Selena Gomez while walking the red carpet at the 2013 ESPY Awards.

The athletes finally have a chance to sightsee after the ten days of competition! The unevenness of the Great Wall made it hard for me to keep my balance, but I still went with a group to walk along a section of it.

THE MOMENT I FAILED

How does it feel to have failed? You didn't do what you said you would." It seemed as if every reporter was asking me that same question. The answer was simple. It felt awful. Like a punch to the gut. Like I let everyone down, especially myself. The funny thing is, I had just won another Paralympic medal! In my second Paralympic Games in Beijing, China, I had taken the bronze medal in the hundred-meter breaststroke. I would be on the podium, taking a prize some athletes work for their whole career. I should have been happy. The problem was that I had told everyone I would walk out of the Beijing Games with seven gold medals, and this bronze medal just killed that dream.

My dad used to tell me about Mark Spitz and his record of seven gold medals at the 1972 Summer Olympics in Munich (West Germany). I figured, *Why not go for seven gold medals—just like Mark Spitz?* I had been ranked first in the world in six events and second in one event. I truly believed with my entire being that I could do it. Months before the competition, I wrote "7 gold" everywhere. I had it written on my laptop screen saver, next to my mirror, and in my journal. I taped a number 7 above my bed so it was the first and last thing I saw each day. I wanted seven gold, and I told that to anyone who would listen. I was more determined than ever before.

Athletes who are about to compete wait in the "ready room." You arrive twenty minutes prior to your race, and if you miss roll call, you are disqualified. Being in the ready room can be quite intimidating. You are surrounded by all your competitors,

Diving into the 200 IM (short course) in Brazil for the 2009 World Championships.

IN THE ZONE

There are a couple of things I do every race day that have become important rituals for me before I feel ready to swim. One of those things is eating a banana. I've been doing this since Athens, where all I had before winning my first gold medal was a banana. I also clap my hands three times and shake my arms out while I'm standing behind the starting block before a race.

just waiting to swim. People are warming up, stretching in corners; some stare at you with a determined look on their face. But most are quiet, listening to music through their headphones. I have always loved dancing. I go into the ready room, put on my headphones, and try to relax by jamming out. I was ready for my first race. I was ready to win and be one gold medal closer to dominating all seven of my events. The thought of anything but a gold hadn't even crossed my mind.

I don't think I had ever cried in front of my mom. I stubbornly refused to cry when most people would—not when I fell, had a bad leg infection, was in pain from a tough surgery, or even when my appendix burst. I used to tease my mom for crying so easily at movies or about other people's struggles. I saw crying as weakness, and I refused to be weak.

But when I went up to the stands as I did after each medal ceremony, this time with a bronze medal in hand, I collapsed in my mom's arms and sobbed. I remember sitting in an empty stairwell with my family, hiding from the fans who wanted to take pictures with me, and crying my eyes out. I wasn't supposed to win a bronze.

I, Jessica Long, was the world record holder. I didn't know what happened. I kept analyzing how my stroke had been slightly off that morning, but I believed it would work itself out and my fastest time would come back for finals. My family was so supportive and genuinely proud of me, but to my sixteen-year-old mind, I was a failure.

I gave up a lot for swimming. I missed out on vacations, birthday parties, weddings, and simple pleasures such as hanging out with friends and doing normal teenage things. I made those sacrifices to be the best in my sport. I was always at the pool, on my way to the pool, talking about a past practice set I swam, or thinking about what crazy set may be thrown at me in the future. My mind was preoccupied with swimming, and I *chose* that. But it didn't mean it wasn't hard to tell my friends every week that I couldn't hang out because I had swim practice, or to turn down that ice cream everyone else was eating, or to skip a family vacation because a competition was coming up and missing even a single day of practice would throw my body off. Suddenly all these sacrifices were staring at me in the form of a bronze medal. I wondered if it had been worth it. Maybe that's melodramatic, but touching that wall in third place absolutely crushed me.

I earned medals for six out of my seven races at the 2008 Paralympic Games in Beijing, China. My dad tried to convince me to be excited about receiving a full set (gold, silver, and bronze), but I only liked the four gold medals.

All ready for homeschool prom in Baltimore, Maryland.

Swimming was my whole world. It's where I found my very self, and it became the way I measured whether I was worthy enough. I had set the foundation of who I was on winning seven gold medals. When I came home with four gold, a silver, and a bronze, it didn't feel like enough. *I* didn't feel like enough. I even considered retirement, all because of a silly color on a medal.

I still loved swimming, but I wasn't sure if I wanted to train for any upcoming Paralympic meets. I got back into the routine of my regular life and started taking college courses along with my homeschool work. I decided to invest more in my social life, having more sleepovers and getting invited to several proms with my friends.

I talked through my doubts about swimming with my coach, Andrew Barranco, who had actually been training me since I started swimming. He refused to let me quit. He started picking me up for morning practices at 5:30 a.m. At the end of the summer he sat me down for a one-on-one meeting, where he walked me through my progress and potential. I can always count on Andrew's loyalty and his commitment to seeing me succeed. He has always been willing to train me when I was in the process of switching coaches, or just hear me out when I need to talk. The thought of disappointing Andrew was greater than that of disappointing my parents. He had put up with a lot of sass from me over the years, but he never backed down. I needed that. I always knew I had to put in at least as much work as he put in to my training. I struggled with the decision to get back into the water after the Beijing Games, but Andrew helped me see that I couldn't give in just yet. I knew I needed to compete in the London Games in 2012.

Sporting my Beijing medals in a photoshoot following the 2008 Paralympic Games.

9

THE MOMENT I CLAIMED MY INDEPENDENCE

When I look back on my life, the years I spent at the Olympic Training Center (OTC) in Colorado Springs were some of the best. As my high school graduation was quickly approaching, I felt that I needed a change. Since I had already turned professional, I decided the training center was the right place for me to be challenged and grow as an athlete. The Olympic Training Center is basically a Disneyland for athletes.

It's this amazing facility where Olympic and Paralympic hopefuls can live and train full-time. It's impossible not to become a better athlete while training there. For swimmers, there's a beautiful fifty-meter pool, a hot tub and a cold tub for recovering, and really anything you would need. One of my favorite places at the OTC was the Sports Medicine Clinic, where the staff would work on my shoulders after practice and I could get massages whenever I wanted.

And then there's the food! The food in the cafeteria is some of the healthiest and most delicious in the world. They use whole foods and lean meats, with no processed sugars in sight. Avocados were traded like gold, and you had to know the right people to get one. Waffle Sunday was always my favorite day in the OTC cafeteria. After a long week of training, having a giant waffle was the perfect way to end the week.

At my homeschool graduation! I was extra excited because I was asked to speak as valedictorian.

I was eighteen, and the OTC was essentially my college experience, although instead of attending classes, I went to countless swim practices and weight training sessions, yoga and Pilates, and sports medicine. I had the opportunity to try new sports, too, and I was always happy to meet all the athletes outside of the swim world and hear about what made them passionate about their sport.

In 2010, I graduated from high school, competed in my second World Championships in the Netherlands, explored Paris for a few days with my two best friends, Kelley Becherer and Anna Eames, and from there went to my new home in Colorado Springs.

I had been attending swim camps there since I was twelve, but on my first night there as a resident, my suitcase still packed from Worlds and Paris, I was scared. This was where I would be *living*. This was it. I was on my own. That night I went out to get pizza for dinner, and it was my last taste of cheesy, greasy food for a long time.

I swear the first few weeks were designed to kill us . . . either that or the altitude really got to me. The OTC, based in Colorado Springs, is 6,557 feet above sea level and is meant to create a more difficult training atmosphere. Some days I'd be winded from just walking from my room to the pool. All I did during those first few weeks was eat, sleep, and swim. It was intense and exhausting, and I loved every second. I loved competing with the other Para-athletes, and I didn't want to let my new coach, Dave "Davo" Denniston, down. In fact, during the second week, I didn't even tell my coach I had bronchitis, because I didn't want to miss a single practice.

I worked hard on my room to make it feel like a home away from home. I had a huge zebra picture above my bed, a bunch of circle mirrors strategically placed on one wall, and blackout curtains to block the sun for my recovery naps between practices. My only job was to swim—and swim fast. I quickly learned that the workouts would only get harder. We had something called "hell week" every month, where our practices would intensify and we were all pushed to our limits both mentally and physically. At the end of each hell week, my friend Anna Johannes and I would treat ourselves to a chocolate feast at the Melting Pot. Sometimes, looking forward to that tradition was the only thing that kept me going during hell week.

My dad took this picture of me diving into a race. I've been blessed to have such a supportive family who tried to come to as many swim meets as they were able to.

I will never forget my coach's birthday. Davo Denniston had been my teammate in Beijing, and now he got to yell sets at me on a daily basis. On his thirty-second birthday he made us swim a main set of thirty-two 200s at an all-out sprint. That is 6,400 meters of pure pain in less than two hours. I went directly to my bedroom afterward and crashed until I had to get up for weights. Our weight-training session wasn't much easier. For one hour, my team and I cycled through a circuit workout nonstop. At each station we had one minute to do whatever workout was in front of us, and this went on for one long hour, with the "Happy Birthday" song playing in the background. After that workout, dripping in sweat, our weight coach Amanda took my whole team out back, where Davo was casually sitting on a lounge chair in the bed of a white pickup truck. He was holding a fancy drink and wearing a silly birthday party hat. His idea of a birthday treat was for us to push the truck around the entire OTC. Every time he blew his whistle, we had to sing "Happy Birthday" to him. Once we got back to our original spot, he surprised all my teammates and me by taking us out for ice cream instead of making us swim our second practice. I was exhausted, and my aching shoulders were so thankful for a break that I almost cried.

TYPICAL DAY AT THE OTC

6:30 a.m.: *Walk to the pool, stretch, change, and mentally prep for practice.*
7:00 a.m.: *Jump into the pool.*
9:00 a.m.: *Climb out of the pool.*
9:15 a.m.: *Relax muscles in hot tub.*
10:00 a.m.: *Head to "the caf" for breakfast.*
11:00 a.m.: *Nap.*
2:00 p.m.: *Start weight training.*
3:00 p.m.: *Finish weight training and grab a snack.*
3:30 p.m.: *Start second swim practice (usually full of sprints).*
6:00 p.m.: *Eat dinner.*
7:00 p.m.: *Get a massage from Sports Medicine and work out shoulders.*
8:00 p.m.: *Do yoga.*
9:30 or 10:00 p.m.: *Fall into bed.*
6:15 a.m.: *Wake up and do it all over again!*

It was always hectic, but I couldn't imagine a better place. There were so many amazing things at the training center. Lining the walls leading to the pool are pictures of all sorts of athletes with their medals. Inspired by these strong individuals, I wanted to get my picture up there too. (My picture ended up being added after London, and I was so excited!) The OTC became my home, and the people there became my second family. Flower, the cook, knew my egg order before I arrived at the grill; I went to movie premieres with my teammates; on Easter we had a huge egg hunt across the entire campus; and we had game nights and planned other fun outings together.

My favorite day of the week was Sunday. Not only was it Waffle Day, but we had the day off from training, which made everyone happy. I'd spend hours in the cafeteria, talking with my friends and teammates. Despite our different backgrounds, we all had similar goals and were training hard for London. The Olympic Training Center was exactly what I needed at that time in my life, and Colorado easily stole my heart. I really grew up during my time there. Colorado gave me my confidence back. I knew I was training harder than anyone I would be competing against, and I was as prepared as I could be for the moment I would step onto the block in London 2012.

Permanently a part of the Olympic Training Center in Colorado Springs.

10

THE MOMENT I FIRST SPOKE TO A CROWD

I have always been a fan of challenging myself to try new things and accomplish new goals. Public speaking scared me, but when I was about fourteen and the opportunity came to present a twenty-minute speech about my story, I decided, *Why not?* Agreeing to speak was one thing . . . and then came the preparation. To be honest, my dad wrote the speech, but I still had to practice it and learn how to be comfortable in front of an audience. I'm an audible learner, so my dad recorded the speech for me to listen to over and over so that I could memorize the whole thing. My dad was an elder at our church, so he had a set of keys to the building. For about six weeks, twice a week, I went to our church to practice my speech. My dad would drive me over after swim practice or on my day off. We turned on all the lights in the sanctuary and I took my place at the pulpit.

We would turn the microphone on so I could learn not to be afraid of my own voice. My two younger sisters occasionally came with us and sat in the pews to listen to me speak. My dad is someone I have always admired and looked up to. He is endlessly kind, selfless with his love, and committed to his children. He is also one of the most patient people I've met. I didn't want to disappoint him. We worked together on how to connect with the audience, and he taught me how to "work the crowd." He showed me how to appear relaxed as I used the stage, pausing at certain points and flashing a charming smile at others. Even with his help, I still had the entire speech printed out word for word because I was too nervous to just speak from some note cards.

My mom helped out too. She took me shopping! I remember going out with my mom, first to lunch and then to find the perfect businesslike outfit. This was during my "rebel against my parents" phase, so I never told her how much I enjoyed these one-on-one dates of ours. I chose a black sweater with blue-and-black-plaid dress pants. I loved it! I felt just like a professional speaker.

When the day of the speech came and I finally shared my story, it was incredible to experience how much the crowd appreciated what I said. I was only fourteen, but I had been through many challenges and had experienced a lot. I knew my life was unique, but I didn't realize how much it could inspire people.

Many individuals came up to me afterward and told me what an impact my story had had on them. I received such positive feedback that I decided I wanted to give more speeches. I have now presented countless speeches—in front of hundreds and thousands of people. One of the largest groups I spoke to was in Mexico in 2014 for the Worldwide Meeting on Human Values. More than six thousand people attended, and an additional eighty thousand viewers watched the live video stream. Asked to be the keynote speaker, I spent the entire summer working on that speech with my sister Hannah. She typed my thoughts and assembled them into a cohesive forty-five-minute presentation. I'm grateful for every opportunity to share pieces of my story and for the things I've learned from people along the way. I wanted my audience to realize that you always have a choice to give in or keep going. All my life I have had to make the daily decision to keep going and to avoid giving up in difficult times. I want to encourage others to do the same. God gave me a story to share, and that is what I intend to do.

In my first and only beauty pageant as a child. This was the beginning of my love for fashion shows.

THE MOMENT I FIRST MODELED

I have always loved being in front of the camera. When I was little, I used to get all dressed up and have my little sisters take pictures of me in our backyard.

After I started winning medals, professional photo shoots were such a treat. I would pose with my gold medals and work my angles and just have a lot of fun. As much as I adore swimming, I'll admit that modeling interested me first. I've watched every season of *America's Next Top Model* and imagined what it would be like to be one of those girls. And now, swimming has given me the opportunity to actually be a model.

My first high-fashion modeling experience was for *Elle*. I am the only amputee they have ever photographed for the magazine, so it was an even more meaningful experience for me.

My best look, by far (LOL). My sisters and I were playing dress-up and I threw a shirt over my head to make my "hair" longer and finish off this stunning ensemble.

The photo shoot was in L.A., and a whole team was there to get me ready. They started with my hair, even adding hair extensions; they applied my makeup to perfection and gave me a manicure. I had never felt so pampered and glammed up. Ralph Lauren provided the clothes for the shoot. The stylist picked a deep purple dress and paired it with my high-heel legs. My "sexy legs," as I call them, have the feet* molded with a four-inch arch so they can be worn only with high heels. A typical shoot lasts about four or five hours, and I loved every minute of it. I wanted the photographer to see that I, a girl without legs, could be a great model. I knew how to position my body, and I wanted to give them lots of options. One of the poses we did was with my legs up on a wall to show off my prosthetics. I really loved the way they allowed me to showcase who I was—a girl without her legs, which for most people would be a big deal. I want to help change the mentality of the fashion industry. I want to show everyone that our differences are what make us beautiful and unique. *Elle* decided to use a picture of me on a couch, posing on my knees without my prosthetics. The photo was risky, and the magazine received a lot of great press about it. It was really cool to be a part of something that showed how people with disabilities can do the same things as everyone else, including model.

FASHION TIPS:
I'M ALL ABOUT
COMFY-CUTE.
I LOVE SIMPLICITY—
SKINNY BLACK
JEANS WITH A
WHITE V-NECK
TEE, A FLANNEL
SHIRT, AND LOTS OF
BOHEMIAN RINGS.

One of my favorite pictures of me at seventeen years old. I made one of my sisters be the photographer, and we had a photo shoot in our backyard.

Some photo shoots have been more stressful. When a number of people are directing your movements very specifically, it can get a bit nerve-racking. I generally ignore my legs because I don't want people around me to be focused on my "disability" or treat me any differently, but it's a balancing act walking around in prosthetics. I've ripped holes in many a pair of jeans over the years from falling. Thankfully, everyone is always willing to work with me, and I've had only great experiences at my photo shoots. I'd like to thank Tyra Banks for all her tips through *America's Next Top Model* and for teaching me how to "smize" (smile with your eyes). The hours I spent watching her show have definitely paid off.

*My high-heel legs, or "sexy legs," were created using my sister's feet. Hannah came with me to meet my prosthetist at A Step Ahead Prosthetics in New York, and there they molded her feet at a four-inch arch and used those molds to make my prosthetic feet. The new legs were then airbrushed and painted to look real, complete with veins and freckles. I love getting to wear my sexy legs to fancy events and am always amazed at how real they look!

12

THE MOMENT I FELL IN LOVE WITH SWIMMING ALL OVER AGAIN

I honestly felt no pressure going into the London Paralympic Games. I didn't announce my exact goals for London. I didn't want people to be disappointed if my performance didn't meet their expectations. Only my coach, Davo, and I knew what goals I had set for myself. Athens was a discovery of what I was capable of, Beijing was the pressure to be the best, and London was my time to have fun.

Competition day three of the Paralympics in London, England: competing in the Women's 100m Breaststroke heats at the Aquatics Centre.

September 6, 2012, in London. Celebrating my gold medal from the Women's 100m Freestyle on the podium at the 2012 Paralympic Games.

Some of my best friends. JAK (Jessica, Anna, and Kelley) for life.

On the cover of the daily magazine at the London 2012 Paralympic Games.

I had already won seven gold Paralympic medals, and I didn't feel that I had anything to prove to anyone. My hope for London was to perform well, but also to enjoy the little moments, such as when our team would all stand together chanting "U.S.A!" for our teammates. I wanted to enjoy my last chance to room with my best friend, Kelley Becherer, who was planning to retire from the Paralympic world six months after London. I was there to do what I loved . . . swim. I had trained hard for four years in prep for London, and I wasn't going to rush through the ten days of competition.

A typical day of competition in London was hectic. I'd wake up around six a.m., head to the cafeteria to grab breakfast, and take the shuttle to the pool. I'd put on my practice suit and go straight for the competition pool to warm up, then over to my trainer, Brian Bratta, to be stretched out and have my back adjusted. Then I'd put on my competition suit, which can take up to forty-five minutes because it's ridiculously tight, fitting like a second skin in order to provide the least resistance in the water. Following a quick warm-up, I'd wait in the ready room for my race. After the race, I'd cool down, get out of my suit, head back to the village, eat lunch, take a nap, and prepare for the finals. Then back to the bus station to repeat all that for finals. After finals (which could end as late as ten p.m.) I'd rush to get dinner, unpack my swim bag, and get to bed, ready to do it all over again the next morning. By day four of competition I was exhausted, but the training had conditioned me to push through it.

Overall, London was my favorite Paralympics. They did a phenomenal job hosting the Games. There were crazy crowds cheering us on every night, the medals were the biggest I've ever won, and the food provided in the Paralympic village was amazing. You could always find me at the fruit and pasta stations.

Nastia Liukin, me, Michelle Kwan, and Allyson Felix at the Women's Sports Foundation Gala in New York City. It's amazing getting to know these elite athletes. They are strong, beautiful, incredible women.

FAVORITE SNACKS:
ALMONDS AND TURKEY JERKY!

It was an honor to put on my Team USA clothing every day and represent my country. At the closing ceremony, Coldplay, Rihanna, and Jay-Z performed. It was the perfect ending to my third Paralympics. I left London having earned five gold medals, two silver, and one bronze. I of course had wanted faster times and wasn't completely satisfied with my performance, but I was proud of what I accomplished, and I had a blast doing it.

At an event for Liberty Mutual, signing autographs and showing off one of my gold medals from London.

THE WHITE HOUSE

This was taken while working on Michelle Obama's campaign against childhood obesity. I was so nervous going through my lines, but she was the kindest person!

June 15, 2012

Ms. Jessica Long
U.S. Olympic Training Center
1 Olympic Plaza
Colorado Springs, Colorado 80909

Dear Jessica:

It was a pleasure to meet you at the U.S. Olympic Committee Media Summit in Dallas, and I hope you know how thrilled I was to have you join me in our *Let's Move!* Olympic Public Service Announcement.

As you know, improving the health and wellness of our Nation's children is one of my defining missions as First Lady. I truly believe our PSA will shed light on this important issue, and through collaborations like these, I know we can help build a brighter, healthier future for our next generation.

Thank you, Jessica, and I wish you the best of luck as you represent our Nation in London.

Sincerely,

Michelle Obama

13

THE MOMENT I LOST MY CONFIDENCE

Although the London Games were a success, nothing could prepare me for the months that followed . . . What happened literally changed the course of my life. While training for London, I had begun receiving emails, tweets, and Facebook messages about a family in Russia. Reporters were claiming that they had found my biological family. They wanted me to come to Moscow after competing and reunite with this so-called family on a TV talk show. Here I was, preparing for a huge competition, trying to remain focused, while completely blindsided by news of this family—the family I had always dreamed of meeting but never expected to hear from. I later learned that the U.S. Olympic Committee, my family, and my agent were all receiving messages about my Russian family. They had decided to wait until after the Games to tell me. They had no clue that I had been exposed to the news and was already trying to deal with it.

I will never forget walking back to the USA building in London and overhearing some woman with a Russian accent saying, "We found Jessica Long, we've got her." She then handed me a note with a phone number on it and information about where to meet my Russian family. I was so overwhelmed. I didn't know what to believe or what I should do with this information. I decided to focus on competing and deal with all of this when I got back to the States.

When I first got back home to Baltimore, I spent a day sleeping, relaxing, and catching up with my family. The next day, we received an email with a link to a Russian television talk show. The program introduced my biological parents. It was surreal to view this family claiming to be my family. I had a Russian friend help me translate some of it, but I didn't know what to feel. I didn't know how to act. All I felt was confusion.

Still, part of me had to admit that I was fascinated. I learned that this was my real biological family, my mother had married my father, and they had three other children together: Anastasia, Dasha, and Oleg. I was the oldest, but my sister was less than two years younger than I was. I even received a Facebook message from Anastasia. She wrote that she heard about having an older sister when she was eight years old, and she had planned to come find me when she could. I was used to the idea of my Russian mother, but the thought of having a biologically related little sister was incredible to me. I can honestly say I loved her right away. It took me a while to get used to the idea of having a father and two other siblings, who are twins. The whole thing was just hard to wrap my head around.

Once all the excitement from London had subsided, my life mostly returned to normal. I took about six months off to travel for appearances, and I kept myself too busy to deal with my emotions.

I didn't really know how to address my new family in Russia. I became a little detached from the idea of them. I think being a professional athlete is partly to blame for the way I can hold my emotions in check. In swimming, during a tough set, we have to push through and ignore any pain we feel. I did that when it came to my Russian family. I wish I had shared more of what I was feeling with my friends and loved ones. I had so many questions about my new family; there was so much I wanted to know: Why did they give me up? Did they love me now only because of my swimming success? Did they ever want me or think about me? I think the quote "Overthinking leads to negative thoughts" is a pretty accurate description of what was going on with me at that time. Swimming has always been the place where I clear my head, but not this time: I would think nonstop about my Russian family.

On top of all that news, I was going through a classic case of post-Paralympic depression. I had spent the last four years of my life training for London. Everything builds up to the competition, and then it is over. Just like that. The event I had spent so long visualizing, working toward, and focusing on was finished. I struggled a lot in the months following London. In truth, I wasn't sure what I wanted to do next.

14

THE MOMENT I FOUND PEACE

I was raised in a Christian home where God was always at the center of my family. We prayed together before meals and read Bible storybooks before bedtime. We went to Cub Hill Bible Presbyterian Church every Sunday morning, and Christian music was a staple in my house. I went to youth group and Bible studies when I could between training, and I attended Vacation Bible School in the summertime, which I loved. My parents never forced any of their beliefs on me. They taught me the Bible and encouraged me to ask questions and seek a relationship with God at my own pace. I always had trouble with schoolwork and struggled with comprehending information, and I had the same issue in this area. I hated that all my siblings seemed to have an easy faith while I struggled to piece it all together. I prayed, not fully understanding and not fully convinced.

Most times in my life, my fire and independence were good things. They moved me forward and kept me motivated. But those same traits caused me to consistently push God and the church away. I wanted control. When I was younger, I couldn't put this into words, but I now realize that I never felt good enough. I was used to working to be like everyone else and fighting to be on top of my sport. People were telling me that the love of this perfect and all-knowing God was a gift I could just accept, that I didn't have to work for it. I wasn't buying it. I didn't fully understand how God could really love me when I didn't always like myself. I wanted to believe, but why would Jesus Christ sacrifice himself and care about what was going on in my life? It just didn't make sense.

Posing with my dad at my cousin's wedding! I have a plethora of cousins, so there's pretty much always an engagement, wedding, or baby shower being planned.

It wasn't until I made the move away from my parents that I really started to question my relationship with Jesus. I could no longer go along with my parents' and siblings' faith when I was confronted with things that opposed it every day. It was as if I had all those years to study Christianity, and now it was time for me to take the test and see if any of it had stuck. I was constantly torn between the morals and beliefs I was raised with and the way everyone I was surrounded by thought and lived. I started pushing God further away so I didn't have to be different. Thankfully, I have an amazing family, who kept me in their prayers, and a God who is faithful in His pursuit and never let me get too far away.

I started having severe anxiety, and the OCD* tendencies I always had came at me with full force. Once, I spent so long making my bed to perfection—ironing wrinkles out of it, lint-rolling it, and laying every corner just so—that I slept in the empty room of my suite (my roommate had moved out) for the next six months so I didn't have to mess it up. I became obsessive over my weight and diet, and I started forcing myself to throw up if I felt that I ate too much on a particular day. My struggle eventually manifested itself as panic attacks, and I was rushed to the hospital by ambulance twice because the attacks were so bad that my friends thought I was dying. I thought so too. I felt as if my body were being ripped apart from the inside. Once, I was so sure I was having a heart attack that I called my mom to say goodbye.

While I was struggling through all of this, I found a church in Colorado that I really loved. I met some awesome people there, and I was reintroduced to the idea of personally choosing Jesus for my own life. I still fought against it, even as I was questioning and pursuing more answers for myself. After London and all the emotions that came with learning about my Russian family, I was so overwhelmed that I couldn't really feel anything. I knew it was time to let go. It's easier to give up control when you realize you never had control over life anyway.

That summer, everything began to change for the better. One night at my church's young adult Bible study group I actually felt God tug at my heart. In that moment, I made a vow to actively pursue Jesus, and I finally felt like I was enough. I realized that God doesn't promise to make everything better, but He promises to be with me in every moment and every circumstance, ready to cover me in His endless grace. Becoming a Christian didn't mean that everything would be easy-breezy from there on out, but in my moments of doubt, I can draw on my faith to face each new challenge that life brings.

*Obsessive-compulsive disorder (OCD) is a common, chronic, and long-lasting disorder in which a person has uncontrollable, repeated thoughts, urges, or mental images that cause anxiety (obsessions) and repetitive behaviors (compulsions) in response to an obsessive thought. I personally have to keep things in perfect order and am constantly cleaning my apartment and my Jeep.

15

THE MOMENT I RETURNED HOME

From the time I was a little girl, I always wanted to train with the North Baltimore Aquatic Club (NBAC) at the Meadowbrook Aquatic Center. The team's coach, Bob Bowman, has trained many Olympic swimmers, including Michael Phelps and Allison Schmitt. The commute had been a bit too long for my parents while they were juggling the activities of their other kids, so I competed with teams closer to home, pushing NBAC to the back of my mind. After the London Games, while I was still at the Olympic Training Center, I started to wonder if I could go back and swim with what had always been my dream team.

I was scheduled to speak at Boston College in April, and it turned out that Bob Bowman was the other speaker. I could tell how passionate he was about coaching. While sharing a ride to the airport with him, I decided it was the perfect opportunity to ask what he thought about me training with him for the U.S. Olympic Team Trials. He gave me his card and said that the next time he was at the OTC, we could have a chat about the possibilities. A month later he and his team came to train at the OTC and I was invited to Baltimore to swim with Bob's team at NBAC.

I knew the first six weeks at NBAC would be the hardest—at least, that's what I kept telling myself. I have never trained so much and so hard in my life. It's a whole new ball game training with Olympians as opposed to Paralympians, but I had to do it. I had to prove to myself that I could keep up with able-bodied Olympic swimmers. London was over, I was avoiding thinking about my newly found family

Overlooking my home: Baltimore.
I love getting coffee and then climbing this hill to take in the view.

in Russia, and I needed a new goal.

At every practice with NBAC, I had to give 110 percent. If I gave anything less, I would not make it through the grueling sets. My life was literally eat, sleep, swim. But I loved being able to throw myself back into training.

HERE'S WHAT A DAY WITH NBAC LOOKS LIKE:

5:45 a.m.: *Alarm goes off. Roll out of bed, grab swim bag, and drive the four minutes to the pool.*

6:00 a.m.: *Arrive at the pool, begin stretches.*

6:45 a.m.: *Meet with Bob and the team to go over our workout, goals, or info on upcoming meets.*

7:00 a.m.: *Swim first practice of the day—a good seven thousand to eight thousand meters, long course.*

9:00 a.m.: *Weight training with the girls.*

10:00 a.m.: *Nap.*

12:00 p.m.: *Get up, have coffee and a snack.*

2:00–4:00 p.m.: *Swim second practice, covering six thousand to seven thousand meters. (Once, we swam eighteen thousand meters in one day!)*

8:00 p.m.: *Climb into bed*

I formed some incredible friendships with my teammates. In fact, I met my two best friends at NBAC. You get to know what people are made of when you endure one grueling practice after another. I remember the day after Thanksgiving in 2014, when we had a practice called the Turkey Burner. There are only a few practices I can point to that made me cry. This was one of them. I was the last person out of the pool when it was over. I walked over to my legs, and Michael Phelps took one look at me, knelt down to my level, opened his arms, and gave me a big hug. It was nice to be surrounded by people who knew exactly what you were going through. NBAC was the most tight-knit swim team I have ever been part of. Even on our day off, after seeing one another nonstop all week for fourteen-plus workouts, we chose to spend even more time together as friends.

It's funny how those moments of struggle turned out to be some of the best memories—those times when I could have given up but kept going and pushing myself. I trained so hard that I barely had time to think about anything beyond surviving each practice. The hardest decision each day was whether I should gather up the strength to eat something or immediately drop into bed for a nap. When I look back on those intense workouts, I see that I didn't know if I would make it through. But I kept going back, and I felt I was where I needed to be.

The prettiest place in the world.

All bundled up with Hannah in Russia.

16

THE MOMENT I RETURNED TO RUSSIA

Before my Russian family contacted me, I had actually been talking with a documentary film producer who was interested in helping me find my biological mom. In 2013, things were put on hold as we tried to figure out how to tie in my Russian family with the documentary we were working on. It seemed that I'd never meet my family. Then NBC approached my agent and said they wanted to film the reunion. They offered to provide transportation and security, take me to the orphanage where I was adopted, and accompany me to visit the home of my biological family. I immediately said yes, and I decided to take my younger sister Hannah along with me for the trip. She knows exactly how to handle my unique way of dealing with emotions, and I completely trust her advice. As my little sister, she is supposed to look up to me, but I always find myself looking up to her.

On December 8, 2013, Hannah and I made the trip from Baltimore to New York to meet with the NBC crew and travel to Moscow. It was the first stop on our long journey. Leading up to this trip, I tried to remain very calm. I didn't think too much about what I was about to do. I continued swimming, and I packed as if I were just packing for another swim meet, except with more fleece-lined clothing. I tried to keep my feelings neutral. We landed in Moscow and had a five-hour layover. Just before we were about to board our next flight to Irkutsk, the plane was delayed for another seven hours. The explanation was simple: "This is Russia," followed by a shrug of the shoulders. We later discovered that those words were the common reply to any question that had an unexplainable answer.

We were finally able to board our plane for Irkutsk, and when we arrived at our hotel, Hannah and I went straight to bed. We were exhausted from more than thirty hours of traveling. Hannah dropped off immediately, but I quickly realized that I wouldn't be getting much sleep. I woke up at one point and checked the time to find that it was only 1:30 in the morning. My mind kept racing, and I decided I needed to clear my head, so I went to the gym and worked out for three hours. I came back to the room, showered, and watched a TV show, all while Hannah slept peacefully. In case you were wondering, she slept for a healthy thirteen hours.

After breakfast, along with the NBC crew, we drove an hour to the orphanage that had been my temporary home all those years ago. This was such an amazing moment for me. As we walked into the orphanage, caretakers, cameras, and children were everywhere, and they were so excited to meet me! They gave me flowers and led me to several different rooms full of babies and young children. Normally, small children don't seem to respond well to me, but these little ones ran right up to Hannah and me and threw their arms around our legs with huge smiles on their faces. They just wanted to be held and loved.

Setting up to record an interview with NBC for the documentary "Long Way Home: The Jessica Long Story." We had to leave the hotel room door open, and our sound guy nearly had a heart attack every time someone stomped by with their suitcase in the hallway.

At the orphanage where I was adopted. Thankfully, they've moved to a newer building since my adoption. This adorable baby was so smiley while I held him!

I was able to meet the woman who had handed me over to my adoptive father in 1993. She remembered meeting my dad and asking him what my American name would be. After spending a few hours visiting the different rooms, I went outside to answer questions for NBC. We did small interviews whenever we had any free time.

Hannah and I both stood outside the orphanage, processing all we had just witnessed and trying to convince ourselves not to adopt all of these children and bring them back home with us. Visiting that orphanage and meeting so many beautiful children helped me realize how much my family in Baltimore loves me. I always had a hard time comprehending and processing the love my adoptive family gave to me as a child. Even though I am not a biological daughter to Steve and Beth Long, they love me unconditionally, and in that moment I could finally see it clearly.

Once we left the orphanage, we boarded a train on a journey that would take eighteen long hours. Somehow Hannah and I managed to power through with the help of books, hot chocolate, and lots of laughter. We arrived in Bratsk late in the afternoon the next day.

FAVORITE BOOKS:
THE SUMMER I TURNED PRETTY TRILOGY.
I HAVE READ ALL THREE BOOKS IN THE
SERIES, EIGHT TIMES EACH!

The mayor met us at the train station with a giant bouquet of pink roses and escorted us to our hotel. I walked into the hotel lobby to find a crowd of kids and parents waiting for me. They asked questions and gave gifts, and one girl even recited a poem. I felt so welcome everywhere I went in Russia. After signing autographs and talking to the group, Hannah and I went to our room to unpack and prepare for one of the biggest moments of my life . . . the day I would meet my Russian family for the first time.

This is the woman who handed thirteen-month-old baby Jess to my dad when he went to the orphanage to adopt me. She remembered asking him what my name would be and him replying, "Jessica."

17

THE MOMENT I MET MY RUSSIAN FAMILY

I can't fully express what I was feeling that early morning. I had been waiting for twenty-two years to meet my birth parents, and in a few short hours I would be reunited with them. There was so much I wanted to say, but more than anything, I wanted to make sure my mother knew I wasn't angry or upset at her for giving me up for adoption. I don't know what I would have done as a teenager in her place, with no money, a disabled baby, and nowhere to stay if I kept her. I think she was really brave. I wanted her to know I forgave her and that I was grateful to her for giving me life.

We all packed into a van and, after a three-hour drive, arrived at my Russian family's house. The NBC crew went inside ahead of me so they could set up cameras and equipment for the shoot. Hannah and I waited almost an hour in the van outside their house. It was torture. I had been waiting for what felt like forever for this moment. It was surreal and totally bizarre to be outside, knowing they were just yards away.

Finally Matt, the director from NBC, came back to the van and told me that when Hannah and I were ready, we could go and meet my family. The media was absolutely insane. Russia One news station had bodyguards guarding my parents' property to keep the other stations' reporters from getting too close. We had NBC cameras, Russia's Channel One news cameras, and a bunch of other Russian reporters surrounding the property. There were even a couple of cameramen on

This was such a special moment between my mom and me. I left my coat inside, so she wrapped hers around my shoulders and then kissed me on the cheek.

The home where my family in Russia lives and where I went to meet them.

neighboring rooftops, all trying to capture the moment I would meet the woman who gave birth to me.

Walking around the house to the back door, I was mainly hoping that I didn't slip on the ice. I held Hannah's arm tightly as we glided down the icy sidewalk. As we walked alongside the house to the back, we could hear my mother and sister crying through the thin walls. When we turned the corner and they came out the back door, my mom immediately came over and hugged me. She was sobbing by then, and there was a special moment when I was hugging her and she was holding and kissing my face. The thought came to me, *This is my mom.* It was a beautiful moment I'll never forget.

My mom had prepared a lunch for us to enjoy together, so we all sat around the table and I was able to talk with my family through our translators. I could ask all the questions I had been storing up for a lifetime. It turns out that my mother had hoped to go back for me when I was three years old, but I had already been adopted.

After we ate, I got to see pictures of my parents and siblings growing up. I was given a picture of my mother when she was seventeen, the year she was pregnant with me. I took off one of my prosthetics and showed them my leg (or my nub, as I like to call it) while my mother just held my hand and gazed at me, as if trying to fathom that I was real.

Anastasia, my mom, and I compared faces in the mirror and discovered that we all have the same green-and-gold eyes. We took tons of pictures together, and Hannah made sure my makeup wasn't smeared all over my face from crying. Thank the Lord for waterproof makeup!

It's crazy to think about the life I might have had if the Longs hadn't adopted me. Whether I was adopted by a different family or had stayed in Russia and never had my amputation or access to prosthetics, I doubt I would have found swimming and the Paralympics. I am so thankful that God had a plan for that little Russian orphan. I wouldn't want my life to have played out in any other way.

Meeting my sister Anastasia for the first time.

Two worlds collide. My American sister and my Russian sister meet.

Right after receiving my gold medal in the Olympic Aquatics Stadium.
My heart was so full.

18

THE MOMENT I FINALLY WON GOLD IN RIO

After the emotional roller coaster following my reunion with my birth family, my life slowly returned to a fairly regular routine, filled with training, family, friends, occasional speeches and appearances, and more training. I set my sights on Rio and counted the days until what would be my fourth Paralympic Games.

Three years later, in 2016, I'm at Rio and my world is shattering. It was the ninth day of a ten-day competition, and I still hadn't won a gold medal. I had been winning golds since I was twelve years old. How could this be possible? These were races I had won since I was a new swimmer, events in which I had taken first place my whole life, competing only against myself, attempting to beat Paralympic and World records that *I* had set. Now I was coming in second, third, or even worse. It hit me heavy and it hit me hard. I let myself cry alone in my room and then did my absolute best to pick myself up and swim my fastest in the next event. Each day got harder and harder as I was more exhausted and

more discouraged by my performance. Day nine came and went, and I had three silver and two bronze medals to my name, but not a single gold. On the very last day of competition for my final race I knew I had just one more chance to stand in the center on the very top of the podium. I was going to have to race my heart out.

My childhood coach, Andrew Barranco—who had been hired onto the Paralympic coaching staff and coached me in Beijing, London, and now Rio—pulled me aside. "You've got this," he said. He never doubted my abilities and was always there whenever I needed help. This race was my last opportunity, not just for myself, but for all the people who supported me through everything and were cheering me on. There were so many people rooting for me. I wanted to prove to everyone that I could still win gold as a twenty-four-year-old in my fourth Paralympic Games. But *I* needed this too. I wanted to win gold for all of us.

On day ten, my last day of competition, I had the two hundred IM (individual medley). The IM includes fifty meters of each of the four strokes—butterfly, backstroke, breaststroke, and freestyle—so you have to be strong in

On the field at M&T Bank Stadium at a Ravens game. Baltimore will always be my home.

Visiting my family in the stands after winning gold. They were always decked out in USA gear and even had matching #TeamLong shirts and sweatshirts made by Arena (my sponsor for swimwear).

Sporting my Rio gold medal and red carpet attire at the 2016 Team USA Awards.

each stroke to earn a medal. Coming into the wall on the last lap, my very last chance to earn a gold medal, I reached out and hit the side in first place. I immediately sobbed. I climbed out of the pool and lay on my back on the pool deck. I couldn't breathe, but I didn't care. Everyone was applauding, and even as the rest of the deck was cleared, the officials all let me have my moment. I finally stood up, and the entire crowd cheered again. It seemed that everyone knew what I had gone through to get that medal, and it was one of the best moments of my life. I now had my Rio gold medal, giving me a combined total of twenty-three Paralympic medals, thirteen of them gold, and making me the second-most decorated U.S. Paralympian of all time.

19

THE MOMENT I ACCEPTED ME

There are still days when I struggle with the *whys* of my life. Why this happened or that happened. But the fact of the matter is . . . I was given *this* life. Even though all these obstacles have been thrown at me, I choose to look at my life in a positive way. If I wasn't missing my legs, I may not have found swimming.

I certainly wouldn't be a member of the U.S. Paralympic Swim Team, and I wouldn't have made the lifelong friendships I found along the way. I know God has a purpose for me, and that He is always there to help me pick up the pieces when I'm overwhelmed. There will always be days when I wonder why, when I wish everything were different—days when I just want to give up. But I've chosen not to let the adversities in my life defeat me. I've chosen not to let swimming, my disability, my past, or some gold medals define me.

I don't have one specific moment when I accepted who I am. I have struggled with acceptance and understanding throughout my entire life. Every challenge I've faced has taught me how to accept my differences as I constantly create who I am each day. As a little girl, I was really insecure about the fact that I didn't have my lower legs. It bothered me when people stared. It made me feel that there was something wrong with me. It has taken me years to realize it was my own insecurities that caused people to treat me differently. If I view my disability as a negative aspect of my life, I'm basically inviting others to view it the same way. I'm giving them permission to feel sorry for me by feeling sorry for myself. But I refuse to be

Basically me in one picture: a coffee in my hands, brick wall for pictures, and wearing my favorite shoes.

defined by what makes me different. I am in control of the way people see my disability. Sure, people will always notice when I wear clothing that shows off my prosthetic legs, but it no longer holds any power over me.

In a lot of ways, I think swimming prepared me for many moments in my life that have been completely unrelated to sports. Swimming teaches you to push through challenging sets; it teaches you success and how to rise when you've fallen down. It taught

Posing with the palm trees in the Cayman Islands.

me how to deal with good and bad pressure, how to set goals and reach them. It has helped shape me into the person I am today. Swimming has been my life's work. Sometimes that terrifies me, and I wonder where I'll go from here, but I'm willing to figure that out when the day comes. I regret nothing—not one practice or race. I missed out on many aspects of what is considered a normal life because of competitive swimming. I skipped parties, couldn't hang out with my friends. I missed weddings and family vacations. I was homeschooled, though I loved the idea of going to an actual school. I gave up eating certain things so I could keep my body in shape. I lost friends. But I found a vital piece of myself, too. God knew what He was doing when He led me to the water. It's where I found my passion, my challenges, my aspirations, my job, and my dreams all in one.

There is a life beyond swimming. I don't know what my future holds, but I'm looking forward to finding out. What about you? What does your story look like so far? Will your next chapter be a continuation of the last, or do you need to tear up the previous one and start a completely new story? Whatever moment is next for you, I hope you

On my balcony at the Olympic Village in Rio.

remember my journey. Remember not to let anyone hold you back, including yourself. Take whatever glimpse of an opportunity you can get and run with it, because you are worth it. Give the best of yourself to each and every moment, because it's your hard work and grace in the daily challenges that prepare you to be unsinkable in the big moments.

We are all writing our stories. I've shared moments from mine in this book, but I have many more moments to go. I'm ready for my next chapter... as ready as I'll ever be.

Date night at Boordy Vineyards with my boyfriend, Lucas!

acknowledgments

THROUGHOUT MY ENTIRE LIFE I have had nothing but love and support from my family, and with this book they continued to be there every step of the way. I am honored to be sharing life with so many incredible people. This truly wouldn't have been possible without them.

First and foremost, I have to give credit to my sister Hannah. I'm so thankful for her brilliant mind and the way she's able to capture my deepest thoughts. There was no one else I wanted to write this book with. Thank you for ALL of your hard work, H. I love you!

A huge thank-you to my dad for the countless hours he spent sorting and scanning pictures, and to my mom for always picking up the phone and listening to me talk about the book over and over again. Their boundless love for each of their children will always amaze me.

I am forever grateful to my agents, Heather Novickis at Kinetic Group Sports Management and Sandra Bishop at Transatlantic Agency, for the continuous work they put into this entire process.

Thank you to our editors, design team, and every individual at Houghton Mifflin Harcourt who helped bring this book to life and put it into readers' hands.

And, of course, my endless gratitude goes to Jesus. Without Him my story wouldn't be anything. He is always worth it. "The Lord is my strength and my shield; my heart trusts in him, and he helps me. My heart leaps for joy, and with my song I praise him." —Psalm 28:7

photo credits

Author's collection: 9, 13, 16, 18, 19, 20, 21, 23, 24, 25, 26, 28, 29, 30, 31, 33, 34, 35, 37, 40, 41, 43, 45, 46, 47, 48, 50, 51, 52, 55, 57, 59, 62, 63, 65, 67, 70, 71, 72, 73, 76, 78, 81, 83, 84, 86, 89, 91, 93 (bottom), 94, 95, 96, 97, 100 (left), 101, 102, 103 (left), 105, 106, 108, 109, 110, 112

IAN MACNICOL: 68, 69

Instagram @zpotler; website: zpotlerphotography.com: 99, 100 (right), 103 (right)

Joe Kusumoto Photography: 11, 38, 42

NBC SPORTS / SAMSON CHAN: 92, 93 (top)

Photo by Living Radiant Photography: 66, 111

Roy Cox, Photographer: 53, 64

Seeing my family and boyfriend after my races in Rio always brought a smile to my face.

photo gallery

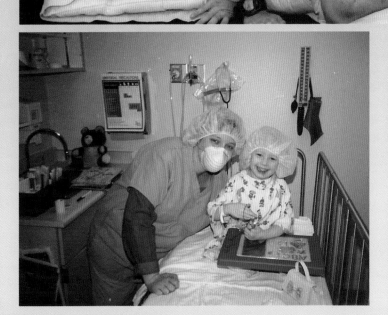

To Jessica Long
With best wishes,